```
B           Littwin, Mike
VALEN
ZUELA       Fernando Valenzuela


$11.93                          2981
```

DATE		
FEB 19 98		

MORNING CREEK ELEMENTARY SCHOOL
10925 MORNING CREEK DRIVE SO.
SAN DIEGO, CA 92128

© THE BAKER & TAYLOR CO.

Sports Stars

FERNANDO VALENZUELA

The Screwball Artist

By Mike Littwin

CHILDRENS PRESS, CHICAGO

Cover photograph: George Robarge
Inside photographs courtesy of the following:
George Robarge, pages 6, 21, 22, 25, and 27
Glenn Feingerts, pages 9 and 33
Ira Golden, pages 11, 29, 35, and 41
Creative Intrusions © 1982 O.C. Shaw, pages 14, 16, 18, and 42

Library of Congress Cataloging in Publishing Data

Littwin, Mike.
  Fernando Valenzuela, the screwball artist.

  (Sport stars)
  Summary: A brief biography of Fernando Valenzuela, a player for the Los Angeles Dodgers who, at twenty years of age, was the youngest player in the major leagues and also one of the best pitchers in the world.
    1. Valenzuela, Fernando, 1960-   —Juvenile literature.
2. Baseball players—Mexico—Biography—Juvenile literature.
[1. Valenzuela, Fernando, 1960-   . 2. Baseball players]
I. Title. II. Series.
GV865.V34L57 1983   796.357'092'4 [B] [92] 82-23611
ISBN 0-516-04331-5

Copyright © 1983 by Regensteiner Publishing Enterprises, Inc.
All rights reserved. Published simultaneously in Canada.
Printed in the United States of America.

    4 5 6 7 8 9 10 11 12 R 90 89 88 87 86

Sports Stars

FERNANDO VALENZUELA

The Screwball Artist

Fernando Valenzuela is the youngest of 12 children. He used to play baseball with his six older brothers. They would not let him pitch. They made him play first base instead.

"They thought I was too young," he said.

The Los Angeles Dodgers do not think that Fernando is too young any more. Fernando now pitches for the Dodgers. He is their youngest pitcher. He is also their best pitcher. He is one of the best pitchers in all the world.

In 1981, his first full season with the Dodgers, Fernando was 20 years old. He was the youngest player in the major leagues. But that did not stop him.

He was National League Rookie of the Year. This award is given to the best first-year player. And he won the Cy Young Award. This award is given to the best pitcher in the National League. No rookie had ever won the Cy Young Award before Fernando.

"Age doesn't matter," he said. "There are more important things."

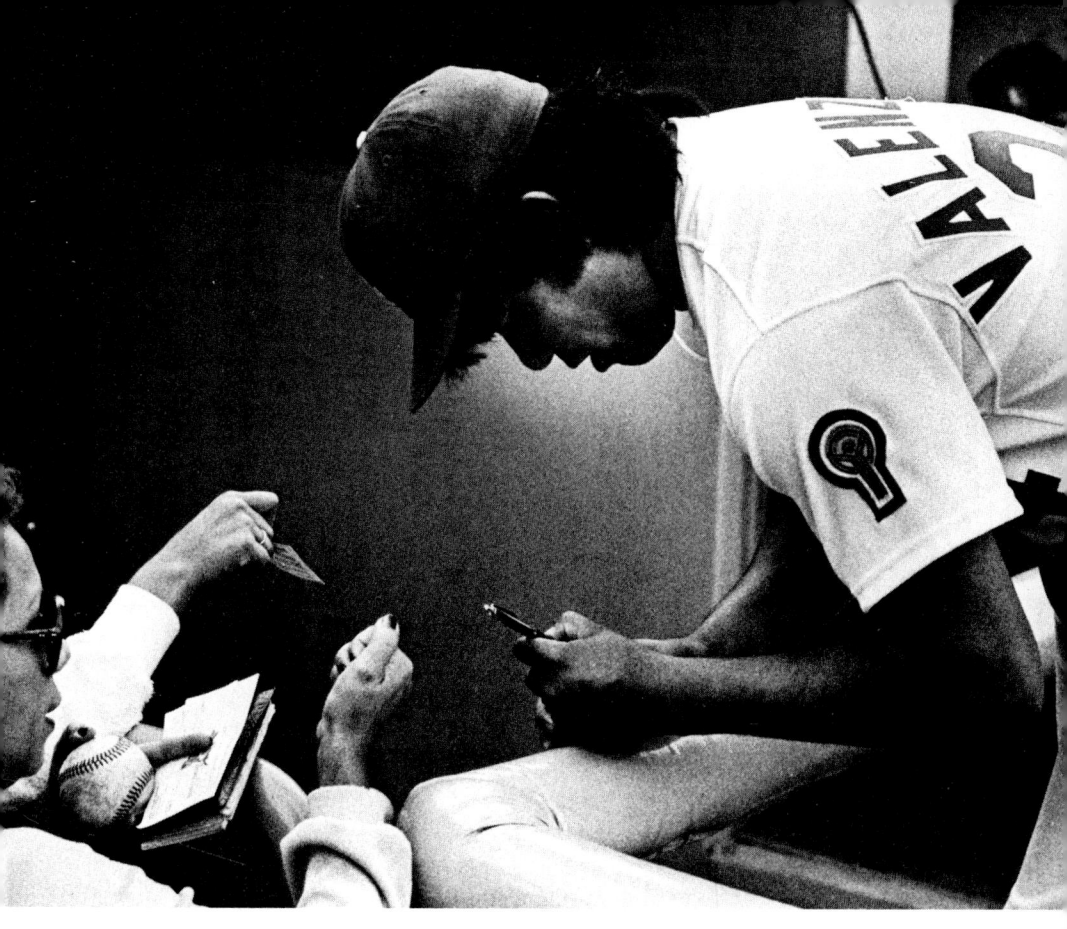

A lot of people did not believe that anyone so young could be that good. So the Dodgers gave out copies of his birth certificate. Fernando was born November 1, 1960, in a little town in northern Mexico.

And now, everyone has to believe Fernando.

"Fernando is a special person," said Reggie Smith, once a teammate of Fernando's. "He was touched by God."

In his rookie year Fernando won his first eight games. Five of those were shutouts. A shutout is when the other team does not score any runs. He won 13 games that season. He helped the Dodgers to become World Champions.

Fernando was famous. They made posters of him. They made records about him. He was invited to the White House in Washington, D.C.

Le Roy Neiman makes a sketch of Fernando.

He met President Ronald Reagan. He was also invited to Mexico City to meet Jose Lopez Portillo, the president of Mexico. In Los Angeles, Fernando was the grand marshall of a parade. About 250,000 people came to watch him.

It all happened very fast for Fernando. But it was not easy.

He cannot speak English. Fernando is a citizen of Mexico, where everyone speaks Spanish. When Fernando talks to people in the United States, he uses an interpreter. An interpreter is someone who can speak more than one language.

When will Fernando learn English?

"I like it better this way," he says. "People can listen to both Spanish and English."

When Fernando was growing up he never thought he would need to know how to speak English. He never dreamed of playing baseball in the United States.

His family was very poor. His village was very small. There was no running water in the houses. Some of them did not have electricity. Fernando's house had four rooms. When he grew up, 17 people shared those four rooms.

"We were poor, yes, but we never lacked anything," Fernando said. "We always had food and clothes. My sisters slept in one room. The boys slept in another."

But Fernando did not always sleep with his brothers. Sometimes, on a warm night, he would sleep outside. And sometimes, when he was scared, he would sleep with his mother.

When he was eight, he began to work in the fields with his father and brothers. But Fernando did not have to work very hard. He was the youngest and his father liked to spoil him.

"I never worked," Fernando said. "I just watched and played. My brothers did all the working."

What Fernando did was think about baseball. He would play every chance he could. Sometimes he would play instead of going to school. He is sorry that he did that now. Fernando's advice to all youngsters is to stay in school.

Fernando played for the town baseball team along with his brothers. When he was 15, he finally got to be the pitcher. He was very good.

"He was a natural," said his oldest brother, Raphael. "Give him a bat and he'll hit the ball.

Give him a glove and he'll play first base. Give him a ball and he'll strike somebody out."

He was invited to pitch in a state tournament. Fernando is left-handed, but he did not have a left-hander's glove. When he went out to pitch with a right-hander's glove, the people laughed. But he struck out the next two batters. The fans began to cheer.

His team won the state championship of Sonora. Fernando was the most valuable player. But when Sonora went to play in the nationals, Fernando was not allowed to pitch. They said he was too young.

Even though he was just 15 he signed a professional contract to play baseball. His mother cried when Fernando left home to play baseball. She thought he was too young to be off by himself.

Baseball was very hard for him. All the other players were much older. And Fernando was very shy. His teammates would call him *muchacho*, which is Spanish for boy.

When Fernando was 18 the Los Angeles Dodgers sent Mike Brito, a scout, to watch Fernando pitch. Brito thought he was a very good pitcher. He asked Fernando if he wanted to pitch for the Dodgers in the United States.

"I'd go to sleep in the jungle, with snakes crawling all around me, to find another Fernando," said Brito. "But, of course, a player like Fernando comes along only once every 15 years."

The Dodgers signed him on July 6, 1979. They sent him to Lodi, California. Mike Brito went to see him as often as he could. Brito had promised Fernando's mother that he would take care of him.

"Fernando was very young," Brito said. "He needed someone to help take care of him."

When the season was over, the Dodgers sent Bobby Castillo, then a Dodger pitcher, to help Fernando with a new pitch. Castillo taught him how to throw a screwball.

Pedro Guerrero, Davy Lopes, and Fernando in the Dodgers dugout

A screwball is a hard pitch to throw. You have to twist your arm so the ball curves away from the hitter. It is a hard pitch to learn, but Fernando caught on very quickly.

"I've never seen anyone pick it up so fast," said Rod Adams, Fernando's first pitching coach with the Dodgers. "He's just a natural. Is there anything he can't do?"

Castillo was surprised at how well Fernando threw the pitch.

"I only taught him because he is left-handed," said Castillo, who is a right-hander. "Otherwise he might take my job away from me."

Fernando never dreamed he would be playing baseball in the United States.

Armed with his new pitch, Fernando went to San Antonio in 1980. San Antonio is a Dodger farm team. Young players there prepare to play in the major leagues.

Fernando pitched well, but he was lonely.

"I didn't know the language or anything," he said. "I watched TV most of the time."

Fernando loves to watch TV, especially cartoons. And he loves to eat, mostly Mexican food and pizza. But most of all he loves baseball.

The Dodgers kept a careful eye on Fernando in San Antonio. They would send Mike Brito to check up on him. The Dodgers needed a pitcher.

They were hoping Fernando would be ready soon.

At the end of that season Fernando was called up to the big leagues to pitch for the Dodgers.

The Dodger players did not know what to think about Fernando. He weighs more than he should. He does not throw the ball that hard. He does not speak English. And no one could believe he was so young.

"If he is 19," said Dodger pitcher Jerry Reuss, "he's the smartest 19 year old I ever saw."

Fernando pitched 17-2/3 innings that year. He won two games and did not allow any earned runs. He helped the Dodgers tie the Houston Astros for the West Division title in the National League.

The Dodgers and Astros had a one-game playoff. The winner would play for the National League championship. Some people thought Fernando should pitch. But the Dodgers thought Fernando was too young. He didn't pitch and the Dodgers lost.

The Dodgers wouldn't make the same mistake again.

In 1981 Fernando began the season with the Dodgers. He was supposed to pitch the third game. But Jerry Reuss, who was supposed to pitch the first game, was hurt. So was Burt Hooton, who was supposed to pitch the second.

So Tommy Lasorda, the Dodger manager, picked Fernando.

No one could remember the last time a rookie had been the opening day pitcher for the Dodgers. But no one seemed very nervous about it. Especially Fernando.

Before the game, Fernando went to the trainer's room and took a nap.

The game was against Houston, the same team that beat the Dodgers the year before. Fernando threw a shutout. He gave up only five hits and the Dodgers won, 2-0.

Fernando was the hero.

"He may be 20," said Bill Virdon, who manages the Astros, "but he pitches 30."

Fernando beat San Francisco next, 7-1, and kept right on winning. In his fourth game he shut out Houston again, this time 1-0.

"He's amazing," said Virdon.

Former Dodger pitcher Don Sutton was the loser that day for Houston. "I hope he comes back down to earth," Sutton said, "or they find a higher league for him."

Fernando jokes with Tommy Lasorda, the manager of the Dodgers.

Fernando didn't lose until May 9. Philadelphia beat him, 4-0.

"He had good stuff," said Tom Lasorda, his manager. "He lost. We knew he would sometime."

That was the year of the baseball strike. In June the players refused to play because of an argument with the team owners. Fernando went home to Mexico. People followed him wherever he went. He was a star in two countries.

The first game after the strike was the All-Star Game in Cleveland. The game matches the best players in the National League against the best in the American League.

People want Fernando's autograph. He is a star pitcher.

Fernando was the starting pitcher for the National League. It was one more thrill in a season of thrills.

There were more. The Dodgers played Houston in a mini-series. The first team to win three games would advance to the National League playoffs.

Fernando pitched the first game. He pitched very well, allowing only one run in eight innings. But the Dodgers lost. He pitched the fourth game, too. He won that one, 2-1.

In the playoffs against Montreal, Fernando lost Game 2. Andre Dawson, who plays center field for the Expos, wasn't very impressed with Fernando. "There's nothing unusual about Valenzuela except that he's a rookie. And he gets a lot of publicity," Dawson said.

But in Game 5, the final game of the series, Fernando won, 2-1. He also knocked in the first Dodger run. It seemed that he was pretty special.

Then came the World Series. The Dodgers hadn't won the World Series in 16 years. They had lost in their last four tries. And they were losing, two games to none to the New York Yankees, when Fernando got to pitch. No team has ever lost the first three games of a World Series and come back to win.

Fernando did not have his best stuff. He gave up four runs. "I thought the earthquake was tonight, they were hitting the ball so hard," Fernando said. But Tom Lasorda, his manager, wouldn't take him out of the game. "I thought about it," Lasorda said, "But I said, this is the year of Fernando."

And so it was. The Dodgers won that game, 5-4, and went on to win the World Series.

He was a champion his first full year. He was rookie of the year. He won the Cy Young Award. He even got married. He was a favorite of the fans and of his teammates.

"How can you not love him?" said Mike Scioscia, his catcher.

Fernando had been living with Mike Brito and his family. But Fernando and his wife, Linda, moved into a place of their own. He also built a bigger house for his parents in Mexico.

The question was, could Fernando do it again?

"I will do my best," Fernando said. "That is all I can do."

In 1981 Fernando was the first player to win both the National League Cy Young Award and the Rookie-of-the-Year Award.

Fernando and Tony Kubek of NBC

That is how Fernando thinks. He tries very hard all the time. He pitches the best he can. Usually that is good enough.

In his second year he won 19 games for the Dodgers. He finished third in the Cy Young voting. Nobody cared how young he was. All that mattered was the way he could throw a baseball.

"He's a special young man," Tom Lasorda said. "He's always the same, win or lose. And he always gives you 100 percent."

Fernando has shown what hard work can do. In just a few years he left his poor village to become one of the most famous athletes in the world.

For the young Mexican, it's a great American success story.

"He should be on Fantasy Island," said Jay Johnstone, a former teammate. "This kind of stuff doesn't happen in real life."

CHRONOLOGY

1960	—Fernando Valenzuela is born on November 11 in Etchohuaquila, Mexico.
1975	—Fernando signs his first professional contract although he's only 15.
1979	
July	—Fernando is signed by the Los Angeles Dodgers.
October	—Bobby Castillo teaches Fernando how to throw the screwball.
1980	—Fernando is called up to the big leagues at the age of 19.
1981	
April	—Fernando pitches the Opening Game of the season and shuts out Houston.
May	—Fernando wins his first eight games before losing to Philadelphia.
August	—Fernando is the starting pitcher in the All-Star Game in Cleveland.
October	—Fernando wins the deciding game in the National League playoffs and his only start in the World Series.
November	—Fernando wins the National League Cy Young Award and Rookie-of-the-Year Award. He is the first player ever to win both the same year. He was 13-7 with a 2.48 earned-run average and led the league in shutouts and strikeouts.
1982	—Fernando won 19 games, finished third in the Cy Young voting and was an All-Star again.
September	—Fernando Valenzuela, Jr. is born.
1983	—In his third season, Fernando has beaten every National League team in the majors.

DO YOU REMEMBER?

Can you answer these questions without looking back in the book? If you need some help, turn to the page number following the question.

1. How old was Fernando during his first full season with the Dodgers? (page 8)
2. Fernando has met two presidents. Who are they? (page 12)
3. What is a shutout? (page 10)
4. What is the Cy Young Award? (page 8)
5. What langauge does Fernando speak? (page 12)
6. In what year did Fernando play his first full season with the Dodgers? (page 8)
7. Why did Fernando's mother cry when he left home to play baseball? (page 20)
8. How many games did Fernando win in his second year? (page 42)
9. What was the first game after the baseball strike? (page 34)
10. What did Mike Brito promise Fernando's mother? (page 22)

What are some things about Fernando that you like?

ABOUT THE AUTHOR

Mike Littwin is a feature writer with the *Los Angeles Times*. He covered the Dodgers when Fernando came into the National League. He has covered virtually every sport and his assignments have included the World Series, the Super Bowl and Wimbleton tennis. Mr. Littwin is married and has one daughter, Angie, who is 8.